HOW DID SLAVES FIND A ROUTE TO FREEDOM?

And Other Questions about the Underground Railroad

Laura Hamilton Waxman

LERNER PUBLICATIONS COMPANY · MINNEAPOLIS

A Word about Language

English word usage, spelling, grammar, and punctuation have changed over the centuries. We have preserved original spellings and word usage in the quotations included in this book.

Dedicated to Yana, a girl of strength and courage

Lerner Publications Company
A division of Lerner Publishing Group, Inc.
241 First Avenue North
Minneapolis, MN 55401 U.S.A.

Website address: www.lernerbooks.com

Library of Congress Cataloging-in-Publication Data

Waxman, Laura Hamilton.
    How did slaves find a route to freedom? And other questions about the
Underground Railroad / by Laura Hamilton Waxman.
        p.   cm. — (Six questions of American history)
    Includes bibliographical references and index.
    ISBN 978-0-7613-5229-7 (lib. bdg. : alk. paper)
    1. Underground Railroad—Juvenile literature. 2. Fugitive slaves—United
States—History—19th century—Juvenile literature. 3. Antislavery movements—
United States—History—19th century—Juvenile literature. 4. Abolitionists—
United States—History—19th century—Juvenile literature. 5. Tubman, Harriet,
1820?–1913—Juvenile literature. I. Title.
E450.W36 2011
973.7'115—dc22   2010009521

Manufactured in the United States of America
1 – DP – 12/31/10

TABLE OF CONTENTS

THE SIX QUESTIONS HELP YOU DISCOVER THE FACTS!

INTRODUCTION

One day in the fall of 1849, a slave named Harriet Tubman, living in Maryland, sang this good-bye song:

When that old chariot comes
I'm going to leave you.
I'm bound for the promised land.
Friends, I'm going to leave you.

To her owners, the song meant nothing. They never paid much attention to slave tunes. But Harriet's family understood her meaning perfectly. She had decided to risk her life for a chance to be free.

That day she snuck out the gate and fled. She didn't have any money or even a map. She didn't know the route from Maryland to freedom in Pennsylvania. She only knew to follow the North Star and head for the Underground Railroad. Like many slaves, she had heard stories and songs about this secret route to the North.

The Underground Railroad wasn't buried belowground. It didn't have tracks or trains. The Underground Railroad was a network of houses, barns, shops, and churches on the way to freedom. Inside these safe places, men and women were ready to feed, clothe, and hide any slave who needed help. Their secret work changed the lives of thousands of slaves. Together they made history. What was life like for slaves in the United States?

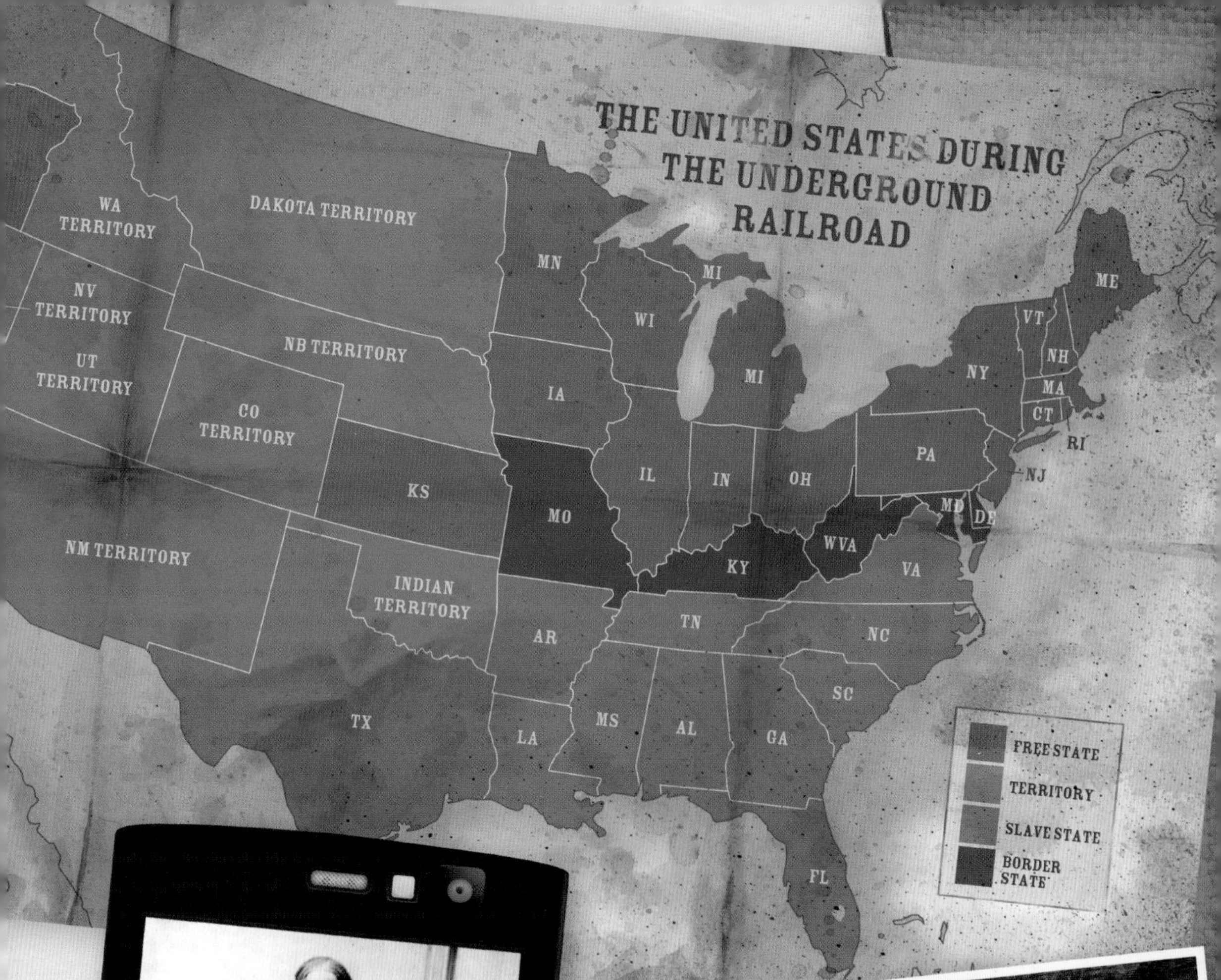

THE UNITED STATES DURING THE UNDERGROUND RAILROAD

WA TERRITORY

DAKOTA TERRITORY

NV TERRITORY

UT TERRITORY

NB TERRITORY

CO TERRITORY

NM TERRITORY

KS

INDIAN TERRITORY

TX

MN

WI

IA

IL

MO

AR

LA

MS

MI

MI

IN

OH

KY

TN

AL

GA

ME

VT

NH

NY

MA

CT

RI

PA

NJ

MD DE

WVA

VA

NC

SC

FL

	FREE STATE
	TERRITORY
	SLAVE STATE
	BORDER STATE

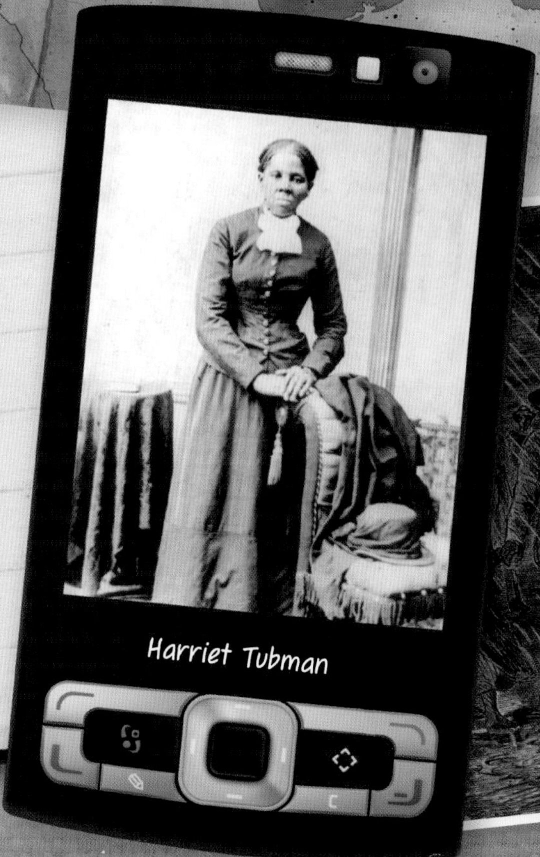

Harriet Tubman

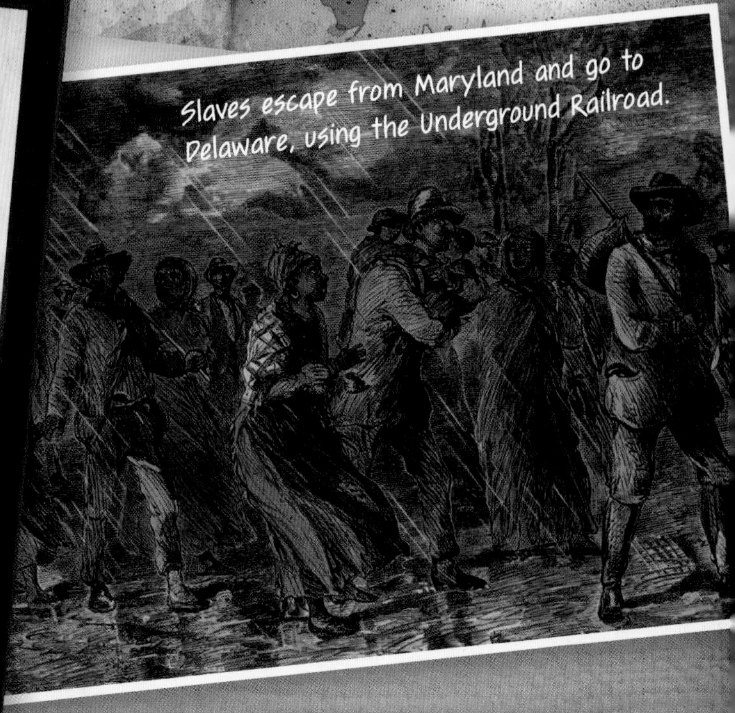

Slaves escape from Maryland and go to Delaware, using the Underground Railroad.

A landowner *(left)* oversees slaves as they work all day picking cotton in this artwork created in the 1800s.

ONE DETERMINED TO BE FREE

Like Harriet Tubman, thousands of other slaves ran away each year. But millions more lived their entire lives in slavery. Slaveholders treated these men, women, and children like property. Slaves could be bought and sold for money. But they couldn't earn any money of their own. They were expected to work from sunup to sundown on plantations and in homes.

In return, they received meager housing, tattered clothing, and barely enough food to survive. They could be whipped or beaten for any reason—or for no reason at all. The cruelest slaveholders cut off fingers,

people who owned one or more slaves. Although nearly all southerners supported slavery, many of them did not have enough money to afford slaves.

large farms in the South

WHEN DID SLAVES COME TO NORTH AMERICA?

Throughout the 1600s and 1700s, European and American traders brought slaves to North America from Africa. Many of them had been dragged from their homes, chained together, and stuffed into dirty, overcrowded ships. The traders then sold them to slaveholders in both the North and the South. By the late 1700s, most northern states had begun to outlaw slavery. And in 1808, the United States stopped allowing slaves to be brought from Africa.

toes, or ears as punishment.

Slaves had no control over where they lived or what work they did. Even worse, they had no power over the lives of their children. Sons and daughters could be sold away from their families without warning. Often they never saw their parents again.

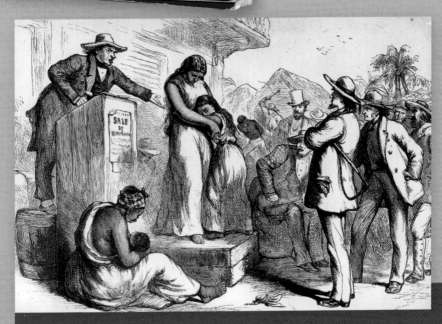

In this artwork created in 1830, a child is being sold at a slave auction.

Slaves pick cotton on a plantation in this artwork by William Ludlow Sheppard (1833-1912).

White landowners in the southern states depended on the work of slaves. Slaves kept their owners' homes and plantations running smoothly. They planted and picked the cotton and tobacco that made many white families rich.

Slaveholders in the South tried to keep their slaves from learning about the North. Southern laws made it illegal for slaves to learn how to read or write. That meant they couldn't read the news or study books. What they learned about the North came from stories and rumors.

Most slaves knew that the northern states had outlawed slavery. Black people there were free. Many slaves had also heard of Canada, a British territory that had also outlawed slavery. But they didn't know where these places were or how to get to them. A slave might live hours or days away from a free state without even knowing it.

Slaveholders who did talk about the North usually spread lies. Slaveholders told their slaves that northerners treated black people terribly. They also said that Canada was much too cold for survival. Said one male slave, "We knew Canada was a good country for us because master was so anxious that we *not* go there." He and thousands of other slaves chose to head for freedom despite the many dangers.

Winter was the most popular time to run away, especially around Christmas. Slaves usually got a few days off for this holiday. A slave who ran away at Christmas might not be missed for several days. Some slaves even got passes to visit family members on other plantations.

HOW DID SLAVES SHARE INFORMATION?

Slaves used songs to spread information secretly about escaping to the North. One of the most famous slave songs was "Follow the Drinking Gourd." To slaveholders, it sounded like a simple folk tune. But it actually gave advice about how to escape from slavery. Using coded words, it explained what time of year to escape, which rivers to follow, and what landmarks to look for. Most important, the song told slaves to always follow the North Star. Slaves and other rural Americans used hollowed-out gourds as water dippers. The *drinking gourd* was a code word for the Big Dipper star formation. It points to the North Star, the way toward freedom.

A slave escapes as slave catchers hunt for him in this artwork created in 1850.

Slaves needed a pass to leave their plantation. Anyone caught without a pass was whipped or beaten. For a slave caught trying to run away, the punishment was much worse. Many captured runaways were beaten to death.

a breed of dog with a very strong sense of smell. Bloodhounds are able to track down animals and people based on scent.

To catch runaway slaves, slaveholders hunted them with bloodhounds. The howling dogs tracked down slaves hiding in woods, caves, and swamps. If a slave couldn't be found, a slaveholder might hire a slave catcher. Slave catchers often chased runaway slaves across state lines.

a person hired to hunt down and capture runaway slaves. These white men often followed slaves from one state to another.

Slaveholders sometimes put ads in their local newspapers. R. Horton of Mississippi

offered fifty dollars to anyone who captured his runaway slave. He said to look for a man who was 5 feet 8 inches (1.7 meters) tall, twenty years old, and wore a gray suit of clothes. These kinds of ads were common in the South.

To avoid being caught, slaves hid during the day and traveled at night. Only under the cover of darkness did they dare to be out in the open. Traveling this way was extremely hard. Runaways had to survive on very little food and sleep. They had to keep moving without knowing exactly where they were going. Often they ended up walking in circles. Sometimes it took weeks or months to get somewhere that was only a few days away.

People escape from slavery in this 1867 painting by Theodor Kaufmann called *On to Liberty*.

Worse than the hunger, the exhaustion, and the confusion was the constant fear of capture. A slave named Josiah Henson described it this way: "A fearful dread of detection ever pursued me. I would start out of my sleep in terror, my heart beating against my ribs, and expecting to find dogs and slave hunters after me."

"I would start out of my sleep in terror, my heart beating against my ribs, and expecting to find dogs and slave hunters after me."

Josiah Henson

These stairs, called the Freedom Stairway, were used by runaway slaves to get from the Ohio River to a stop on the Underground Railroad.

Runaway slaves such as Henson depended on their courage and cleverness to reach the North. Along the way, some of them came across people willing to help. These men and women believed slaves should be free. They opened their homes to runaways and protected them from slave catchers. Over time they came together to form the Underground Railroad.

NEXT QUESTION

WHO **BECAME KNOWN AS THE FATHER OF THE UNDERGROUND RAILROAD?**

Members of the Underground Railroad help a slave to escape in this painting by Arthur Bowen Davies (1862–1928).

TWO THE EARLY YEARS

Isaac Hopper was one of the first people known to help runaway slaves. Because of this, he is sometimes called the father of the Underground Railroad. Hopper was an abolitionist living in Philadelphia, Pennsylvania. He believed that slavery should be abolished, or outlawed.

a person who believed slavery should be outlawed, or abolished

"I would do for a fugitive slave whatever I should like done for myself," Hopper once said. "If he asked my protection, I would extend it to him. . . . If he was hungry, I would feed him. If he was naked, I would clothe him. If he needed advice, I would give him such."

a person who runs away or tries to escape

Hopper began his work around 1797, a few years after the U.S. Congress had passed the Fugitive Slave Act of 1793. This law gave slave catchers the right to capture a fugitive in any free state. The slave catcher simply had to prove to a judge that the captured person was a runaway slave. If the judge agreed, the slave would be returned to the owner.

U.S. Congress: the lawmaking body of the U.S. government

Hopper helped captured fugitives win their court cases and keep their freedom. He also hid them from slave catchers. He was one of the first people to move fugitives from one safe place to another. By the time a slave catcher discovered a fugitive's hiding place, Hopper had already moved the person to another safe, secret location.

Hopper also used decoys to trick slave catchers. The decoy was a person who looked like the hidden fugitive. When the decoy ran out of the house, the slave catcher chased after him. Meanwhile, the real fugitive slipped out the back door. By the time the slave catcher realized his mistake, the fugitive was long gone. This trick was later used by other people on the Underground Railroad.

decoys: people used to draw attention away from someone else

Isaac Hopper

"If he asked my protection, I would extend it to him."

WHERE DID MOST FUGITIVES COME FROM?

Most successful fugitives came from states near the border between the North and the South. That included Kentucky, Maryland, and Virginia. Slaves in states such as Mississippi, Georgia, and Alabama had a much harder time reaching freedom. They had farther to travel. And they found fewer people willing to help. Many of these fugitives were captured before they were able to cross the border to a free state.

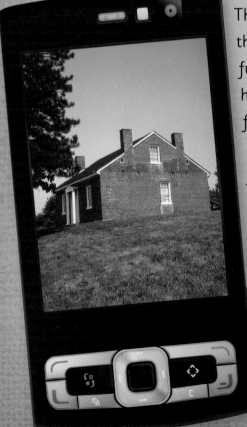

By the 1820s, other well-known abolitionists were helping fugitives in this way. One of them, John Rankin, was a southern minister from the slave state of Tennessee. Rankin's abolitionist beliefs had made him unpopular in the South. He moved to the free state of Ohio in 1822. Rankin bought a home in Ripley, Ohio, a town along the Ohio River. The slave state of Kentucky sat on the other side of the river. Any fugitive coming through Kentucky had to cross the river to reach freedom.

In Ripley, Rankin began hiding fugitive slaves. He lived high on a hill with his wife, Jean, and four sons. Each night he raised

John Rankin's house in Ohio is considered a historical building.

a lantern to the top of a flagpole in his front yard. This glowing light could be seen from across the river in Kentucky. It acted as a guide for slaves making the dangerous river crossing at night. According to fugitive Arnold Gragston, "It always meant freedom for the slave if he could get to this light."

Jean Rankin kept a warm fire and food ready for fugitives who came to the door. After a meal and a short rest, the fugitives had to move on to another safe place. The Rankins soon became famous for helping slaves. Slave catchers from Kentucky often demanded to search their home for runaways.

WHERE IS THE OHIO RIVER VALLEY?
The Ohio River valley is located in Illinois, Indiana, Ohio, western Pennsylvania, West Virginia, and Kentucky.

Newport
Indiana
Indianapolis
Ohio
Columbus
Madison
Cincinnati
Ripley
Ohio River
Kentucky

GPS

This portrait of abolitionists John and Jean Rankin was taken in 1866.

John Rankin's work enraged southerners across the border. They attacked his property and tried to set it on fire. They offered a reward of twenty-five hundred dollars to anyone willing to kill him. But Rankin and his family continued to help fugitives year after year.

About the same time, Levi Coffin, a Quaker, was also helping to hide fugitive slaves. Coffin grew up in the Quaker community of New Garden, North Carolina.

New Garden was one of the few places in the South where people did not believe in owning slaves. As a young man, Coffin helped his cousin Vestal protect and feed slaves on the run. Sometimes the two cousins had to outsmart slave catchers to keep the fugitives safe. Although the work proved dangerous, Coffin believed he had a duty to fight against slavery.

In 1826 Coffin moved to Newport, Indiana. Although Indiana did not allow slaves, many people there supported slavery in the South. That didn't stop Coffin and his wife, Catharine, from opening their home to fugitives.

When a fugitive arrived in the middle of the night, Coffin would cover all the windows and build a fire. Meanwhile, Catharine prepared a warm meal. At the Coffins' home, fugitives could fill their bellies and catch up on sleep. After a day or two, Coffin helped them get to another safe

Levi Coffin

house farther north. Often he took them in a special horse wagon. The bottom of this wagon had a secret opening big enough to hide one or two fugitives. Coffin also hid fugitives under loads of hay or among boxes. He stopped at nothing to help people on their way to freedom. Coffin guessed that he helped up to three thousand slaves during his lifetime.

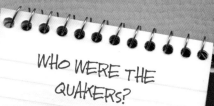

WHO WERE THE QUAKERS?

Like many others on the Underground Railroad, Isaac Hopper was a Quaker. Members of this religion believe that no human being should own another. Quakers refused to own slaves. Quite a few of them opened their homes to runaways. Many people of other religious faiths also took part in the work of the Underground Railroad.

NEXT QUESTION

WHEN DID THE UNDERGROUND RAILROAD GET ITS NAME?

THREE TRAIN TO FREEDOM

When Coffin and Rankin began helping fugitives, the Underground Railroad didn't have a name or an organized network of safe places. Most people who helped fugitive slaves worked independently. They lived across the country in scattered areas and were often unaware of one another. That started to change in the 1830s.

According to legend, a slave catcher first used the term *Underground Railroad* in the early 1830s. He couldn't understand how a fugitive had disappeared into thin air. He wondered if the slave had traveled on a secret railroad underneath the ground.

> a story passed down over many years

Of course, that slave catcher wasn't correct. The fugitive had most likely disappeared into the homes of people willing to hide him. But the name *Underground Railroad* stuck. Abolitionists heard about the story and began using the new term. The story also helped them see themselves as part of a chain of connected people. They called their homes stations. They called themselves stationmasters, conductors, or operators. And they called fugitives passengers on the freedom train.

LIBERTY LINE.
NEW ARRANGEMENT---NIGHT AND DAY.

The improved and splendid Locomotives, Clarkson and Lundy, with their trains fitted up in the best style of accommodation for passengers, will run their regular trips during the present season, between the borders of the Patriarchal Dominion and Libertyville, Upper Canada. Gentlemen and Ladies, who may wish to improve their health or circumstances, by a northern tour, are respectfully invited to give us their patronage.
SEATS FREE, *irrespective of color.*
Necessary Clothing furnished gratuitously to such as have *"fallen among thieves."*

"Hide the outcasts—let the oppressed go free."—*Bible.*
☞For seats apply at any of the trap doors, or to the conductor of the train.
                                        J. CROSS, *Proprietor.*
N. B. For the special benefit of Pro-Slavery Police Officers, an extra heavy wagon for Texas, will be furnished, whenever it may be necessary, in which they will be forwarded as dead freight, to the "Valley of Rascals," always at the risk of the owners.
☞Extra Overcoats provided for such of them as are afflicted with protracted *chilly-phobia.*

This newspaper advertisement for the Liberty Line is a coded reference for a route on the Underground Railroad.

During these years, more abolitionist organizations started springing up in the North. Some of their new members took part in the work of the Underground Railroad. In that way, the Underground Railroad grew larger each year.

Rumors of the Underground Railroad started to reach slaves in the South. By the 1840s, many more slaves were risking their lives to escape. Later, some of them became operators on the Underground Railroad. They were joined by free blacks. Together these men and women played a major role in running the Underground Railroad.

free blacks: African Americans who had bought their freedom from their owners or were born free

In Madison, Indiana, a group of black business owners helped hundreds of fugitive slaves. They were led by George DeBaptiste, a successful barber. DeBaptiste turned his barbershop into an Underground Railroad station. Next door, Stepney Stafford ran a laundry business. He listened for rumors of slave catchers in the city and warned DeBaptiste if someone was about to capture a fugitive in hiding. Elijah Anderson, a blacksmith, then helped the fugitive sneak out of town. Sometimes he took people as far as Levi Coffin's house in Newport, about 170 miles (274 kilometers) away.

William Still was another African American who became famous for his work on the Underground Railroad. Born free in the North, he moved to Philadelphia in the 1840s. There, he organized a committee of black and white abolitionists to help fugitives entering the city. One of the fugitives who came to him for help turned out to be his brother Peter. Peter had been sold to a southern slaveholder when he was a young boy. The family thought they had lost him forever.

In large northern cities such as Philadelphia, Underground Railroad workers like William Still were rarely punished. These cities tended to ignore the rules of the Fugitive Slave Act of 1793. They did not stop people from running the Underground Railroad. And they allowed an escaped slave to live in the area as a free person.

In some towns, working on the Underground Railroad came at a great cost. The black community of Madison, Indiana, was attacked more than once by angry white southerners.

WHO WAS HENRY "BOX" BROWN?

William Still helped hundreds of fugitives fleeing to Pennsylvania. One of the most famous fugitives he came across was Henry "Box" Brown. In 1849 Brown escaped from slavery in a very unusual way. He mailed himself to Philadelphia in a wooden box.

They wanted to scare people into stopping their work on the Underground Railroad.

In Wilmington, a town in the slave state of Delaware, a judge fined white stationmaster Thomas Garrett about eight thousand dollars for hiding slaves. That would equal nearly two hundred thousand dollars in modern money. Garrett probably did not have to pay the entire fine. But he lost his property and nearly everything he owned. Even so, he continued to help fugitives.

Underground Railroad operators in the South faced even worse punishments. In 1845 police arrested Jonathan Walker, a sea captain, for helping about eight slaves escape from Florida. As punishment a red-hot iron was pressed into the skin of his palm. The iron permanently branded the letters *SS* into his skin. The *SS* stood for "slave stealer." Other captured Underground Railroad workers spent years in prison.

branded permanently marked on the skin with a hot iron. Slaves were also branded as punishment.

Thomas Garrett kept a station on the Underground Railroad in this home in Delaware.

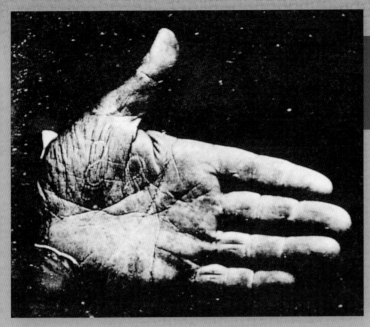

Captain Jonathan Walker had his hand branded with SS—slave stealer—when he was caught assisting fugitive slaves.

The constant fear of being caught took a toll on many of the people who ran the Underground Railroad. Levi Coffin's relative Addison Coffin ran a station in North Carolina. He later said, "The life of anxiety and extreme danger I was leading was rendering me nervous, excitable, and suspicious of all my surroundings; there was a constant sense of danger resting on my heart."

The dangers were great, but the Underground Railroad continued to expand its reach throughout the 1840s. At the same time, more slaves were risking everything to be free. One of them was a woman who eventually would become the most famous Underground Railroad operator of all.

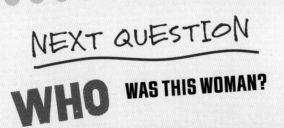

NEXT QUESTION

WHO WAS THIS WOMAN?

Harriet Tubman is famous for her days helping slaves on the Underground Railroad.

FOUR THE FEARLESS HARRIET TUBMAN

Harriet Tubman was born around 1820 in the slave state of Maryland. Little Harriet was a sickly child. Even so, her owner put her to work when she was just five years old. He sent her away from her family to serve a cruel neighbor woman. Instead of paying Harriet, the woman paid Harriet's owner. Harriet did household chores during the day and cared for the woman's baby at night. If the baby's crying woke the woman, Harriet got a terrible beating.

Harriet worked for several other neighbors during her childhood years. None of them treated her with kindness.

She was glad when her owner sent her to work in the fields when she turned eleven or twelve years old. By then Harriet had grown into a strong young woman.

A white overseer watched over her and her fellow

a person whose job it was to keep watch over slaves. Most overseers were white men, but some were trusted slaves.

workers in the fields. He whipped them if they moved too slowly or tried to rest. He also punished them if they tried to leave. One day a field slave sneaked into town. When the overseer found out, he chased after the man. Harriet raced ahead to warn the man that the overseer was after him.

The overseer caught up to the slave and threw a heavy weight at him. It banged into Harriet's forehead instead. The heavy piece of metal hit her so hard that it wedged a piece of her scarf into her skull. Harriet nearly died from the injury. From then on, she had fainting spells. These spells came on suddenly, and they lasted for the rest of her life.

Harriet also began to have visions, or waking dreams. She believed the dreams were messages from God.

In the mid-1800s, an overseer (a work supervisor) weighs bushels of cotton handpicked by slaves. The plantation owners made lots of money by using the free labor of slaves.

In one dream, she saw herself flying like a bird over fields, rivers, towns, and mountains. She flew until she crossed the line into freedom. The dream made her long to be free. But Harriet was very close to her family. The idea of leaving them broke her heart.

In 1849 something happened to change Harriet's mind. In the fall, she learned that her owner planned to sell her. She realized she might never see her family again. She decided to run away.

Harriet had heard of people in Maryland who helped runaway slaves. Somehow she discovered the name of such a person living nearby. Harriet went to this woman's house under cover of darkness. The woman gave Harriet directions to a house that was an Underground Railroad station. The white couple running the station hid Harriet during the day. At night they sneaked her into another town. There a different Underground Railroad worker gave her directions to a farmhouse where she could hide. With this kind of help, Harriet made it all the way to Pennsylvania.

"I looked at my hands to see if I was the same person; now I was free. There was such a glory over everything. I felt like I was in heaven."

HARRIET TUBMAN

A quote from Harriet Tubman is etched on the wall at the National Underground Railroad Freedom Center in Cincinnati, Ohio.

Reaching Philadelphia was a dream come true. "I looked at my hands to see if I was the same person: now I was free. . . . I felt like I was in heaven." At the same time, Harriet felt very alone. "I was free, but there was no one to welcome me to the land of freedom. I was a stranger in a strange land." Harriet made a home in the North, but she missed her family terribly.

While Harriet got used to her new home, the U.S. Congress passed a new law. It became known as the Fugitive Slave Act of 1850. It gave southerners much more power to hunt down runaway slaves in free states. With the new law, black people could be snatched off the streets and dragged from their homes. Many African Americans in the North no longer felt safe.

To protect themselves, hundreds of black families fled the free states. Some of them had been living in freedom for years. They were forced to leave behind houses, businesses, and friends. The Fugitive Slave Act had no power outside the United States. So most of them ended up in Canada. Newly escaped slaves from the South also began heading for Canada.

WHAT WAS THE FUGITIVE SLAVE ACT OF 1850?

The new Fugitive Slave Act was a law that required every citizen to help catch fugitive slaves. Anyone caught protecting a fugitive was punished. The punishment included a large fine and six months in prison. The new law also took away a black person's ability to fight for his or her freedom in court. Because of that, slave catchers sometimes kidnapped free blacks and said they were fugitives. Slave catchers later sold those men and women into slavery.

An 1851 political cartoon depicts the controversy over the Fugitive Slave Act of 1850.

But many fugitives in the North chose to stand their ground. They refused to let the new law scare them. They stayed in their homes and continued to work on the Underground Railroad. White abolitionists also broke the new law by protecting fugitives from slave catchers.

Harriet fought against the law in her own way. In December 1850, she prepared for a rescue mission in Maryland. The husband of her grown niece Keziah, or Kizzy, had sent her an upsetting message. Kizzy was about to be sold away from the family. Harriet refused to let that happen.

Very few fugitives returned to the South. The chances of being captured were too high. Even fewer people entered the

South on rescue missions. The most famous rescuers were three white men named John Fairfield, Charles Torrey, and Calvin Fairbanks. They had all sneaked slaves out of the South. And they had all been captured, arrested, and sent to prison. Harriet knew she was taking a huge risk. She knew she wouldn't go to prison if she was caught. She'd be killed.

Using the Underground Railroad, Harriet led Kizzy, her husband, and their two children to freedom. Eventually they settled safely in Canada. Harriet started thinking about rescuing the rest of her family. She also thought about all the other slaves longing for freedom. "I was free," she thought, "and they should be free also."

Harriet believed that God wanted her to continue rescuing slaves. But that idea scared her. She'd have to risk her life again and again. Surely she would be caught and killed. "Oh Lord," she said, "I can't—don't ask me— take somebody else." But then she thought she heard God say, "It's you I want, Harriet Tubman."

John Fairfield

This painting by Jerry Pinkney (born 1939) shows Harriet Tubman (in blue) escorting slaves into Canada.

Harriet stopped being afraid after that. She began sneaking into Maryland at least once a year. On each trip, she led ten or more fugitives to freedom. She knew the best places to hide and the best tricks for losing slave catchers. She knew how to communicate in code and how to disguise herself. Most important, she knew many secret stations along the Underground Railroad. Her incredible strength, courage, and cleverness never failed her.

Slaves began calling Harriet by the code name Moses. The name came from a famous story in the Bible. In the story, a man named Moses leads thousands of people out of slavery.

Throughout the 1850s, Harriet went on at least nineteen rescue missions. During that time, slaveholders offered huge rewards for her capture. But she never got caught. Neither did any of the people she rescued. In her lifetime, she guided more than three hundred slaves to freedom.

WHAT NAME WAS HARRIET TUBMAN GIVEN AT BIRTH?

Harriet Tubman was named Araminta Ross when she was born. Her family called her Minty. Like many fugitives, she changed her name once she reached freedom. A new name helped fugitives stay hidden from slave catchers. It also carried a powerful meaning. Many slaves had been named by their owners. In freedom they got to choose a name for themselves.

NEXT QUESTION

WHERE DID MANY FUGITIVES CROSS FROM THE UNITED STATES INTO CANADA?

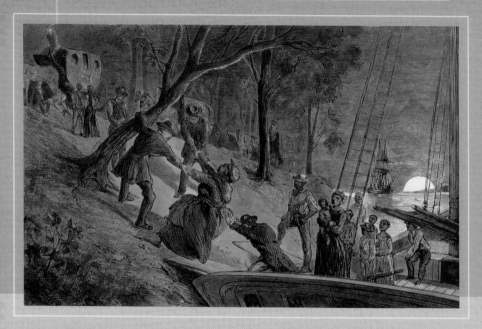

Underground Railroad conductors help fugitive slaves climb up a riverbank in this engraving from William Still's (1821–1902) *The Underground Rail Road Records*.

FIVE THE BUSY YEARS

Like Harriet, many Underground Railroad operators worked hard during the 1850s. Thomas Garrett in Wilmington, Delaware, kept careful records of the fugitives he helped. Between 1822 and 1848, about 56 fugitives came to his door each year. In the early 1850s, he was helping about 75 people each year. By the mid-1850s, about 225 people sought his help each year.

Many fugitive slaves headed straight for Canada. One of the most popular gateways to Canada was Detroit, Michigan. This growing city of twenty-one thousand people sat on the Detroit River. A person could just cross the river

WHAT HAPPENED TO FUGITIVES IN CANADA?

By the early 1860s, about twenty thousand fugitives were living in Canada. Most of them had started out penniless and alone. Over time they found work as shoemakers, tailors, barbers, cooks, farmhands, waiters, and tour guides. Some of them became successful business owners and landowners. Black citizens in Canada also had the right to vote. That right was not given to African Americans in the United States until 1870, with the Fourteenth Amendment.

WHERE IS DETROIT, MICHIGAN?
The city of Detroit is just north of Windsor, Ontario.

on a ferry to arrive in Canada. This mile-long (1.6 km) boat ride became known as Freedom's Ferry.

William Lambert was one of Detroit's black leaders. He helped organize a secret group of Underground Railroad operators called the Detroit Vigilance Committee. Its members hid thousands of fugitives waiting to leave the United States. The group included George DeBaptiste from Madison, Indiana. He had moved to Detroit after white southerners started attacking Madison's black community. Another member of the committee was William C. Monroe, a black minister.

Monroe's church stood five minutes from the waterfront. Many fugitives hid there before crossing the Detroit River.

Another major gateway to Canada was New York State. Underground Railroad stations in the northern part of the state were especially important. From there, fugitives could cross into Canada by boat. Black abolitionist Frederick Douglass ran a station in Rochester, New York. A boat landing on the Genesee River was only 3 miles (5 km) from his house. Every night at eight, a steamboat left from there and headed to Toronto, Canada. In the 1850s, Douglass helped about four hundred fugitives on their way to freedom.

Frederick Douglass

WHO WAS FREDERICK DOUGLASS?

Frederick Douglass was one of the most famous abolitionists in the United States. He had been born into slavery in Maryland in 1818. Unlike most slaves, he learned how to read and write as a boy. Douglass escaped from slavery in 1838. Within three years, he had joined the abolitionist movement. He soon became one of its most powerful speakers and writers. Douglass published a book about his life called *Narrative of the Life of Frederick Douglass, an American Slave*. He also printed the *North Star*, an abolitionist newspaper.

Former slave Jermain W. Loguen was another important New York stationmaster. Loguen had escaped from a cruel owner in 1834. By the 1850s, he was running a busy Underground Railroad station in the northern town of Syracuse. To spread the word, he put an ad in the newspaper. The ad let fugitives know that they could go to him for help. Over the years, more than one thousand people may have come through his door.

In Peterboro, New York, Congressman Gerrit Smith was another stationmaster on the Underground Railroad. This wealthy abolitionist had been fighting for years to end slavery. He also tried to help black people living in freedom. In the 1840s, he had used his own money to buy farms for black families in New York. He believed all people had the right to own land and support themselves.

The Underground Railroad ran through other northern states, including Vermont, Massachusetts, and New Jersey. Routes through Ohio also remained important.

New York congressman Gerrit Smith felt strongly that slaves should be free.

In the 1850s, one of Ohio's most famous stationmasters was Levi Coffin. He had moved from Newport, Indiana, to Cincinnati. By then he had become one of the most well-known stationmasters on the Underground Railroad. Some people even called him the president of the Underground Railroad. But the Underground Railroad didn't have a single leader. It continued to be made up of black and white men and women working side by side as equals.

Coffin worked with many other operators in Cincinnati, including Laura Haviland. She guided fugitives from Ohio to her home state of Michigan. There, Haviland ran a school for both white and black students. This type of school was extremely unusual at that time.

Haviland herself was unusual. Few women, besides Harriet Tubman, worked as conductors on the Underground Railroad. Even so, women were very important to its success. They fed, clothed, and cared for exhausted fugitives. Women also raised money for the Underground Railroad

This engraving from the late 1800s shows abolitionist Laura Haviland holding cuffs and iron slave collars. Slave collars were used to discipline and identify slaves.

ROUTES TAKEN
ON THE
UNDERGROUND
RAILROAD

and sewed clothing for fugitives in need. In Indiana one group of women helped female fugitives hide from slave catchers.

As the Underground Railroad grew busier, so did southerners working against it. Sometimes they sent spies to search out secret stations. If a spy discovered a station, slave catchers later attacked the house. Any fugitive hiding inside would be kidnapped and forced back into slavery.

Once a spy came to Laura Haviland's house in Michigan. He pretended to be a reporter for an abolitionist newspaper. He said he wanted to write an article about how the Underground Railroad worked. Luckily, she turned him away. Haviland later learned that the man had been hired by a slaveholder.

Other spies pretended to be fugitives. These men were slaves or free blacks. Slaveholders paid them to go to the doors of stationmasters, pretending they needed help. Underground Railroad operators invented ways to tell real fugitives from fake ones. In some places, operators gave fugitives coins with notches or holes drilled into them. Fugitives handed these coins to stationmasters to prove they could be trusted. Operators also taught fugitives secret passwords and door knocks.

The Underground Railroad ran throughout the 1850s. And it would have continued were it not for the Civil War (1861–1865). This war was fought between the North and the South. By then many Northerners believed that slavery should be abolished. Southerners believed they had a right

The Battle of Wilson's Creek took place on August 10, 1861, near Springfield, Missouri. It was the first major Civil War battle west of the Mississippi River. The print was created in 1883 by the firm Kurz & Allison.

People in Washington, D.C., celebrate the passage of the Thirteenth Amendment in this illustration by Frederick Dielman (1847–1945).

to keep slaves. But the South lost the war.

The U.S. Congress passed the Thirteenth Amendment to the Constitution. It abolished slavery throughout the United States. About four million men, women, and children gained their freedom at last.

The story of the Underground Railroad remains an important part of our nation's history. It reminds us of what people can accomplish when they work together. About twelve thousand black and white abolitionists worked hand in hand on the Underground Railroad. They helped at least one hundred thousand slaves on their way to freedom. Most of their names have been forgotten. But their courage, strength, and generosity lives on in our memories.

NEXT QUESTION

HOW DO WE KNOW ABOUT THE UNDERGROUND RAILROAD?

Primary Source: *Reminisces of Levi Coffin*

We know about the Underground Railroad from writings of the time. Most of the people who ran the Underground Railroad kept their work a secret. But a few people, such as Levi Coffin and William Still, later published books about the Underground Railroad. These books are important primary sources.

A primary source is a document written by a person who was alive at the time of an event. It is often a firsthand description of something that happened in history. Letters, journals, and newspaper articles are examples of primary sources. The primary source below, *Reminisces of Levi Coffin*, describes how Coffin helped a fugitive who was about to be captured by his owner. At the time, the fugitive was hiding in another man's house in Cincinnati.

> I told the fugitive that he was in great danger, and must change his quarters without a moment's delay. It was then about nine o'clock at night. . . . I sent my horse and carriage to meet him and conduct him to the next depot of the Underground Railroad.

> I was informed the next day that in less than ten minutes after the fugitive left, the house was entered by his master and a posse of men, who had previously discovered his whereabouts. They searched the house thoroughly, but they were too late; they soon realized that their prey had escaped. I might relate many similar instances that occurred in the city. Fugitives were often spirited away when all the preparations for their capture had been made, and their foiled and baffled pursuers continued to search for them after they had safely reached Canada by way of the Underground Railroad.

TELL YOUR UNDERGROUND RAILROAD STORY

You are running a station on the Underground Railroad. You are keeping a secret journal about your experiences. Write a journal entry about your life.

WHERE is your station?

WHO are the fugitives you are helping?

WHEN do they come to your door?

WHY do you believe you should help them?

WHAT do you do to help them?

WHERE do you hide them?

HOW do you get them to the next station?

USE **WHO, WHAT, WHERE, WHY, WHEN,** AND **HOW** TO THINK OF OTHER QUESTIONS TO HELP YOU CREATE YOUR STORY!

Timeline

1619

The first slaves are brought from Africa to what would become the United States.

1777

Vermont is the first northern state to outlaw slavery. Other states in the North soon follow.

1793

Congress passes the first Fugitive Slave Act. It allows slave catchers to cross into free states to capture fugitive slaves.

1796

Isaac Hopper moves to Philadelphia, Pennsylvania. Sometime after that, he begins helping fugitive slaves.

1822

John Rankin moves to Ripley, Ohio, and soon begins hiding fugitive slaves.

1826

Levi Coffin settles in Newport, Indiana, and begins hiding fugitive slaves.

1830s

Abolitionist organizations spring up across the North and bring about the abolitionist movement. The Underground Railroad also gets its name about this time.

1832

The New England Anti-Slavery Society is established.

1834

Jermain Loguen escapes from slavery on Christmas Eve.

1838

Frederick Douglass escapes from slavery in Maryland. He becomes a famous abolitionist and opens a station on the Underground Railroad in Rochester, New York.

George DeBaptiste moves to Madison, Indiana. He later turns his barbershop into an important stop on the Underground Railroad.

1843

Calvin Fairbanks is captured and sent to prison for entering the South to rescue slaves.

1845

Captain Jonathan Walker is arrested for helping slaves. His hand is branded with the letters SS for "slave stealer."

1846

George DeBaptiste moves to Detroit, Michigan.

1847

Levi Coffin moves to Cincinnati, Ohio, and works on the Underground Railroad there.

William Still begins helping fugitive slaves in Philadelphia, Pennsylvania, about this time.

1848

Thomas Garrett is forced by a judge to pay a large fine for running a station on the Underground Railroad. He refuses to stop helping fugitives.

1849

Henry "Box" Brown mails himself out of slavery in a wooden box addressed to Philadelphia, Pennsylvania.

Harriet Tubman escapes from slavery.

1850

Congress passes a tougher Fugitive Slave Act. Fugitives begin fleeing to Canada.

Harriet Tubman goes on her first rescue mission in December.

1861

The Civil War begins.

1865

The South loses the war. Congress passes the Thirteenth Amendment, outlawing slavery everywhere in the United States.

Source Notes

4 Sarah H. Bradford, *Harriet: The Moses of Her People* (New York: Geo. R. Lockwood & Son, 1886), 28, http://books.google.com (accessed September 8, 2010).

9 David W. Blight, ed., *Passages to Freedom: The Underground Railroad in History and Memory* (Washington, DC: Smithsonian Books, 2001), 97.

12 Fergus Bordewich, *Bound for Canaan: The Underground Railroad and the War for the Soul of America* (New York: Amistad, 2005), 118.

14 Ibid., 56.

17 Blight, 112.

25 Addison, Coffin *Life and Travels of Addison Coffin* (Cleveland: William G. Hubbard, 1897), 48, http://books.google.com. (accessed September 8, 2010).

29 Bradford, 30.

29 Ibid., 31.

31 Ibid., 32.

31 Catherine Clinton, *Harriet Tubman: The Road to Freedom* (New York: Little Brown, 2004), 83.

42 Levi, Coffin *Reminisces of Levi Coffin* (Cincinnati: Robert Clarke & Co., 1880), 461, http://books.google.com (accessed September 8, 2010).

Selected Bibliography

Blight, David W, ed. *Passages to Freedom: The Underground Railroad in History and Memory*. Washington, DC: Smithsonian Books, 2001.

Bordewich, Fergus. *Bound for Canaan: The Underground Railroad and the War for the Soul of America*. New York: Amistad, 2005.

Bradford, Sarah H. *Harriet: The Moses of Her People*. New York: Geo. R. Lockwood & Son, 1886. Also available online at Google Books. http://books.google.com (accessed September 8, 2010).

Clinton, Catherine. *Harriet Tubman: The Road to Freedom*. New York: Little, Brown, 2004.

Coffin, Addison. *Life and Travels of Addison Coffin*. Cleveland: William G. Hubbard, 1897. Also available online at Google Books. http://books.google.com (accessed September 8, 2010).

Coffin, Levi. *Reminisces of Levi Coffin*. Cincinnati: Robert Clarke & Co., 1880. Also available online at Google Books. http://books.google.com (accessed September 8, 2010).

Hendrick, George, and Willene Hendrick, eds. *Fleeing for Freedom: Stories of the Underground Railroad as Told by Levi Coffin and William Still*. Chicago: Ivan R. Dee, 2004.

Further Reading and Websites

Evans, Freddi Williams. *Hush Harbor: Praying in Secret*. Minneapolis: Carolrhoda Books, 2008. Simi keeps watch as his family and friends hold a secret prayer meeting. This colorful picture book is based on a true practice of enslaved Africans in the nineteenth century.

Hamilton, Virginia. *Many Thousand Gone: African Americans from Slavery to Freedom*. New York: Knopf Books for Young Readers, 2002. This illustrated book contains true stories about slaves in North America to the end of the Civil War.

Harriet Tubman
http://www.americaslibrary.gov/aa/tubman/aa_tubman_subj.html
Part of the Library of Congress's website, this Web page includes links to information and stories about Tubman.

Moore, Cathy. *Ellen Craft's Escape from Slavery*. Minneapolis: Millbrook Press, 2011. Ellen and William Craft came up with a daring plan to escape from a life of slavery. Did they make their way to freedom?

Naden, Corinne J., and Rose Blue. *Harriet Tubman: Riding the Freedom Train*. Minneapolis: Lerner Publications Company, 2003. This biography tells the story of Tubman's amazing life.

The National Underground Railroad Freedom Center
http://www.freedomcenter.org/underground-railroad/#
This national museum's website is full of information about the history and the people of the Underground Railroad.

Nelson, Vaunda Micheaux. *Almost to Freedom*. Minneapolis: Carolrhoda Books, 2003. A young girl's doll narrates her enslaved family's courageous escape.

Polacco, Patricia. *January's Sparrow*. New York: Philomel Books, 2009. In this novel, Sadie escapes from slavery with her family using the Underground Railroad.

Swain, Gwenyth. *President of the Underground Railroad: A Story about Levi Coffin*. Minneapolis: Millbrook Press, 2001. Learn more about the courageous life of this little-known hero.

The Underground Railroad
http://www.nationalgeographic.com/railroad
This website puts visitors in the shoes of a runaway slave.

Weidt, Maryann N. *Voice of Freedom: A Story about Frederick Douglass*. Minneapolis: Millbrook Press, 2001. This illustrated biography explores the life of this famous black abolitionist.

Index

Photo Acknowledgments

The images in this book are used with the permission of: © iStockphoto.com/DNY59, p. 1; © iStockphoto.com/Skip O'Donnell, pp. 1 (background) and all wooden floor backgrounds; © iStockphoto.com/sx70, pp. 3 (main), 7 (top), 9, 16 (top), 19, 23 (top), 29, 33, 35 (left), 36 (right); © iStockphoto.com/Ayse Nazli Deliormanli, pp. 3 (inset), 43 (left); © iStockphoto.com/Serdar Yagci, pp. 4–5 (background), 43 (background); © Bill Hauser/Independent Picture Service, pp. 4-5, 39, Library of Congress pp. 5 (inset) and 45 (LC-USZ62-7816), 23 (bottom) (LC-USZC4-4659), 30 (LC-USZ62-28755), 37 (LC-DIG-cwpbh-02631); © iStockphoto.com/Andrey Pustovoy, pp. 5 (left), 11, 16 (bottom), 21 (top), 28; 7 Continents History/Everett Collection, pp. 5 (right), 34; © Hulton Archive/Getty Images, pp. 6, 8; © Rischgitz/Hulton Archive/Getty Images, p. 7 (bottom); © North Wind Picture Archives/Alamy, pp. 10, 18, 41, 44; © Wisconsin Historical Society/Courtesy Everett Collection, p. 11 (inset); © Theodor Kaufmann/The Bridgeman Art Library/Getty Images, p. 12 (top); © Kean Collection/Archive Photos/Getty Images, p. 12 (bottom); Ohio Historical Society, pp. 13, 16 (inset), 17 (left), 24, 38; Private Collection/The Bridgeman Art Library, p. 14; © Mary Evans Picture Library/The Image Works, p. 15; © iStockphoto.com/Talshiar, pp. 17 (right), 35 (right); © Bettmann/CORBIS, p. 20; © Chicago History Museum/Archive Photos/Getty Images, p. 21 (bottom); Courtesy of the Massachusetts Historical Society, p. 25; © MPI/Archive Photos/Getty Images, p. 26; National Archives, p. 27; © Mike Simons/Getty Images, p. 28 (inset); Print Collection, Miriam and Ira D. Wallach Division of Art, Prints and Photographs, The New York Public Library, Astor, Lenox and Tilden Foundations, p. 31; The Art Archive/Jerry Pinkey/NGS Image Collection, p. 32; © Stock Montage/Archive Photos/Getty Images, p. 36 (left); © Buyenlarge/Archive Photos/Getty Images, p. 40; The Art Archive/Culver Pictures, p. 43 (right).

Front cover: © Theodor Kaufmann/The Bridgeman Art Library/Getty Images.
Back cover: © iStockphoto.com/FokinOl (background).